OUR TREE

For Lyra,

Knock knock.
Who's there?
Frank.
Frank who?
Frank you for
being my friend!

~ J. M.

tiger tales

A division of Penguin Random House LLC
1745 Broadway, New York, NY 10019
penguinrandomhouse.com
tigertalesbooks.com
First published in the United States 2025
Originally published in Great Britain 2025
by Little Tiger Press Limited

ISBN 978-1-68010-834-7 (proprietary)
Manufactured in China • LTP/1400/5946/0924

10 9 8 7 6 5 4 3 2 1

The authorized representative in the EU for product safety and compliance is
Penguin Random House Ireland, Morrison Chambers, 32 Nassau Street,
Dublin D02 YH68, Ireland. https://eu-contact.penguin.ie

This Imagination Library edition is published by Random House Children's Books, a division of Penguin Random House LLC, exclusively for Dolly Parton's Imagination Library, a not-for-profit program designed to inspire a love of reading and learning, sponsored in part by The Dollywood Foundation. Tiger Tales trade editions of this work are available wherever books are sold.

MIX
Paper | Supporting responsible forestry
FSC® C144853

The Forest Stewardship Council® (FSC®) is a global, not-for-profit organization dedicated to the promotion of responsible forest management worldwide. FSC® defines standards based on agreed principles for responsible forest stewardship that are supported by environmental, social, and economic stakeholders. To learn more, visit www.fsc.org.

OUR TREE

by JESSICA MESERVE

tiger tales

One warm day, Tree
felt the pitter-patter
of tiny feet dash
up their trunk.

It was **Little Red.**

And as he scampered, he chattered,

"This tree is all for

ME."

Tree chuckled,

"**Well, hello!** I'm not

so sure about that.

Look **behind** you!"

There, chomping on
a leaf, sat a teeny,
tiny caterpillar.

"Hey! These leaves are for me!"
puffed **Little Red.**
"And they're not
for eating –
they're for swishing!"

Just one swish later, Swift flew down from the blue sky above. "Such perfect branches for resting on.

Thank you, Tree."

"You're welcome, and sweet dreams," swayed Tree.

"But resting is **boring** and branches are for boinging!" squeaked Little Red. "And, Tree, they're all for **ME!**"

But wise old Tree just smiled. "Look behind you!"

Swift had so
many friends!

"Just a
flying visit,"
piped the birds
in unison.

"How **wonderful** to be together," rustled Tree.

Little Red did **not** agree. "Together is too busy, too noisy, and there isn't space for anyone **else**!"

"Look behind you!" encouraged Tree.

Plodding into view,
Elephant trumpeted,
"What bumpy,
rough bark.

"It's blissful
for scratching on!
**Thank
you, Tree,"**
he rumbled, before
lumbering on his way.

"Good-bye," trilled the birds.

"Good-bye," waved Tree. "Come back soon!"

Little Red was glad they were gone.

"FINALLY, TREE IS ALL FOR . . .

". . . me?"

But from down below and up above, from near and far, more animals, birds, and bugs slithered and swung, crawled and crept through Tree's branches.

Tree welcomed them all.

"We live here together, Little Red. I am for everyone, not just you."

Little Red scowled.

"Well, I'm off to find my own tree," he barked.

"A tree . . .

"that's all . . .

"for ME!"

"Look out!"

called a canopy of voices.

But it was

too late.

Little Red

slipped . . .

. . . and landed on something soft.

Opening one lazy eye, Leopard smiled and licked her whiskers.

"Tree is **perfect** for resting under. So glad you could join me, Little Red.

"But don't you know . . .

"this

tree . . .

"is
for . . .

"ME!

"And so are all the animals in it!" she roared hungrily.

"Are you sure, Leopard?" Tree chuckled. "Look behind you."

Darting from his
hiding place,
Little Red bravely boomed,
"NO, Leopard.
This tree is for
everyone!"

A ROAR filled the air.

But it wasn't Leopard.

Animals big and small
hooted and
howled until . . .

. . . Leopard **yelped** and **fled** over the hills, her ears ringing all the way. The animals **trilled** with **happiness**, and Tree's branches swayed peacefully once more.

Little Red hugged Tree.

"I'm sorry! Please can I stay here with all of you?"

"Of course," Tree smiled.

"But, Little Red, look behind you!

There's someone you should meet."

Before Tree could
say another word,
Little Red scampered
away to play with
his new friend.

Tree beamed.
"So, Little Red, do you still
think I'm only here for you?"

"Of course not," laughed Little Red.
"Tree is for everyone."
This time they ALL agreed.
Life was better
together.